JOHN OF THE CROSS'
LIVING FLAME OF LOVE

Classics for Everyone

Those who turn to spiritual classics for guidance and inspiration often find their style daunting. The original texts still have much to offer but their diction and idiom, chosen for another era and audience, pose an obstacle to many contemporary readers. "Classics for Everyone" aims to make some of the greatest Christian teachers accessible to all.

JOHN OF THE CROSS'
LIVING FLAME OF LOVE

FOR EVERYONE

ELIZABETH RUTH OBBARD

New City Press
Hyde Park, NY

Published in the United States by New City Press
202 Cardinal Rd., Hyde Park, NY 12538
www.newcitypress.com
©2007 Elizabeth Ruth Obbard

First published in 2004 in Great Britain by
New City, London

Cover design by Durva Correia

Library of Congress Cataloging-in-Publication Data:

Obbard, Elizabeth Ruth, 1945-
    John of the Cross' The living flame of love -- for everyone / Elizabeth Ruth
Obbard.
        p. cm.
    ISBN 978-1-56548-267-8 (alk. paper)
    1. John of the Cross, Saint, 1542-1591.
Llama de amor viva. 2. Mysticism--Catholic Church. 3. Catholic Church--
Doctrines--History--Modern period, 1500- I. John of the Cross, Saint,
1452-1591. Llama de amor viva.
II. Title.
BV5082.3.O23 2007
248.2'2--dc22   2007010968

Printed in the United States of America

Contents

For the founding members of
the Community of Our Lady
of Walsingham
"Those who would give light must
endure the burning."

Introduction

Many people think that John of the Cross is a writer and mystic too difficult to understand; therefore they leave him severely alone. It is true that his way of expressing himself is couched in terms that are unattuned to our present day conversational style, but what he has to say is perennially valid. In fact, with very little effort, anyone can read his books and find in them a clear and unambiguous guide to the life of union with God. John is an acknowledged master of spirituality, and in *The Living Flame*, short though it is, we find a complete synthesis of his teaching.

The Living Flame was written when John was forty years old and at the height of his powers. His time of harsh imprisonment was behind him. He held an honored place in the Carmelite Reform and had just been elected superior of the house in Granada, Los Martires. He was also deputed to assist a community of Discalced Carmelite nuns with their foundation in the same city. Among them was Anne of Jesus, with whom he formed close spiritual ties, closer even than his ties with Saint Teresa.

The nuns, unable to find a suitable house for a convent, went to live with a rich benefactress, Señora

Ana de Peñalosa, while a convent was being prepared. Meanwhile John resided at the Carmelite priory of Los Martires, so called because it was situated in the grounds of a former penitentiary, composed of conical shaped underground dungeons, where Christian prisoners had been held during the Moorish occupation. Once a drab and uninviting place, the location had been turned into a lush garden that commanded wide views over the Andalusian countryside. It was a beautiful setting for a religious house, but the building that stood there was small and poor. John himself took over the burdens associated with administration: begging for food when necessary, working as a laborer, overseeing the construction of a viaduct that would bring water to the friars and to the gardens that surrounded their property. Besides this he went regularly to the nuns as confessor and director.

It was at Los Martires that John completed nearly all his writings. He seemed inspired by the beautiful scenery and the knowledge that he had reached the end of a difficult spiritual journey — a "way of the cross" that had taxed his strength, inner and outer, to the utmost. *The Living Flame* was his last work, which he intended to be a gift to his benefactress and friend, Ana de Peñalosa. First he wrote the poem. Later he was persuaded to comment on it, as he had done with the *Dark Night* and the *Spiritual Canticle*. So John took up his pen once more in the midst of his busy life and wrote a commentary in fifteen days, fitting the writing in when he had a few spare moments. Later he expanded and slightly amended the text, but substantially it remained the same. It is the shortest of John's complete works and it contains the fullness of his teaching and experience. In it he sketches not only the way to union with God, but its consummation.

The whole work in essence can be compared to an *Exultet,* an Easter proclamation, coming from one who has passed through death and found, not annihilation but fullness of life. Strong, vital love, a love "stronger than death," is the theme of *The Living Flame.*

The Spirit's mission is to form the Christian into another Christ so that both share the same life principle. As of ourselves we cannot bridge the infinite distance between our life and the life of God; the Spirit comes to initiate and complete the work that we are unable to do. Through the Spirit we are invited to share in God's life, and this is accomplished by a growing union of love.

But to "abide in love" is not natural to sinners who are self-centered. Surrender to a fiery Baptism is the only way. It is this journey that John of the Cross maps out for us.

When we turn to the language John uses, we discover that it is based on metaphors we all know, or think we know: gentleness, loving touch, wounding. It is the love of God the bridegroom, depicted by the prophets in the Old Testament, where Israel is the chosen spouse, destined to belong entirely to her Lord. But there is another language running parallel and equally comprehensible to our human condition. It is the language of devouring passion: the passion of the transcendent God who can brook no restraint. Once passion is aroused, one is swept along to self-loss in the beloved. Ego boundaries dissolve and there is the fusion of two in one. Passion is a relentless fire that burns up all that stands in its way! Love is a roaring fire but it is also glowing candles or lamps. It is a love which spends itself in silent devotion for the other, even in darkness and non-feeling. It is the love of a devoted mother as well as a surrendered spouse.

The language of love is obviously one of superlatives: "You alone are my love.... To you I give all I have and am.... My beloved is mine and I am his.... I will love you forever.... Besides you nothing else matters." While this may sound exclusive, it is not so in reality. John's life of prayer was embraced in the context of a busy schedule as administrator, director, friend, community member. In loving the One who is God we embrace all other people and indeed all creation. For the one in love with God, the fire which invades the soul warms the whole of the cosmos.

While love may open the heart to others, it necessarily implies also a single heart for the beloved. Love of the One means detachment from all the rest, the closing off of other options. But what lover who loves with deep passion and devotion counts the cost when placed in the scales? And was there ever a person who could love two beloveds equally? In some way there is not even a real choice. What are wealth, possessions, esteem, honor, besides love? As Paul says, "I count everything as so much rubbish if only I can have Christ." Love opens up within us depths we did not even know we possessed. We have a capacity for the infinite, and this is what love taps.

Love in essence is difficult to define. We can only know its nature by considering how we express it. Of its nature love is self-diffusive; it cannot be poured into a void. There must be another who receives and reciprocates what is given. A heart-to-heart relationship touches us at our deepest depths. Love enables us to expand; it brings to birth all that we are and can be. It is enrichment, not diminishment.

As the love of Christ was revealed above all in his death, so we must pass with him through the flames of death to resurrection and glory. A relationship of love can exist only where there is likeness — we have within us the capacity to become

Divine. The work of the Spirit is to develop this capacity by wounding (cleansing and purifying) us. This causes us great pain. We have to be hollowed out to receive God; we must hand ourselves over to fire, allow God to reach into depths that we cannot guess at. Only when we are fully purified can we be transformed into another humanity for Christ "from glory to glory."

In *The Living Flame* John hymns this death and new life from the perspective of the latter. With Jesus the soul lets go of her own life, passes through death to self and all self-gratification, so as to receive back in a new way the very life of Christ. Passion may start us on the road, but the goal is the gentle inbreathing of the Holy Spirit, the kiss of love between Father and Son in which we are invited to participate.

In this book John mentions the three classic stages of spiritual growth — a stage of purification in which the soul suffers pain as its impurities are burned away; a stage of transformation when it is gradually configured to the likeness of Christ; and finally the stage of union when, completely purified and transformed, the soul is united to God, sharing the Divine life in an embrace of mutual love. But, unlike most spiritual writers, John starts with the end of the journey and refers backwards, rather than the other way round.

Is it worth all the pain, all the purification? John

would say a resounding "yes." But the way there demands as much generosity as we can muster, for

> Those who would give light
> must endure the burning.

In presenting John's teaching I have simplified the text of *The Living Flame* and omitted some parts of it where John has repeated himself. But basically this book contains all the teaching of his mature years. In it he challenges us, his readers, to be open to a relationship with God that reaches into the depths of our being, transforming us completely. And it was written, not for contemplative nuns, nor even friars engaged in the apostolate. It was written for a laywoman, a widow, with whom John had become friendly. It shows that he felt the way of union was open to all — and that means you and me!

The Living
Flame of Love

Introduction to the Poem
and Its Commentary

• • • • •

Jesus promised that,
with the Father and the Holy Spirit,
he would come and abide in those who love him.
This is accomplished
in the way I shall describe in what follows.

When a log of wood is set on fire
and becomes one with the fire
that is consuming it,
we can draw an analogy
and say that the hotter the fire
the more the log will glow and sparkle and
    emit flames.
In the same way, when the soul is transformed
    in the fire of love,
it is not only united with the divine fire
but becomes itself a living Flame,
glowing and sparkling with love.

This then is its song as it burns with the
    sweetness of love.

O Living Flame of love
That so tenderly wounds
My soul in its deepest core!
As you are no longer painful,
Perfect your work in me if you so will,
Break the web of this sweet encounter.

O sweet burn!
O delicious wound!
O tender hand! O gentle touch!
Savoring of everlasting life
And paying the whole debt.
In destroying death you have changed it
   into life.

O lamps of fire,
In whose splendors
The deep caverns of sense,
Which are usually dim and dark,
With an unusual brightness
Now give light and heat to the Beloved.

How gently and how lovingly
You lie awake in my heart,
Where you dwell secretly and alone;
And in your sweet breathing,
Full of grace and glory,
How tenderly you fill me with love.

Stanza 1

The Song of One Who Has Reached Union with God and Feels the Flame of Love Burning Within

• • • • • •

O *living Flame of love*
That so tenderly wounds
My soul in its deepest core!
As you are no longer painful,
Perfect your work in me if you so will,
Break the web of this sweet encounter.

These are the words of one
who is set all-on-fire with the love of God.
When we are like this
we know ourselves to be separated from God
only by a light veil.
So we can speak to the Flame, which is the Holy
    Spirit,
asking to be taken from this life
in order to experience the joy and glory
    of eternal bliss.

Here the Flame is wounding and touching our
    innermost being,

making us conscious of the Spirit's presence
burning within us like a consuming fire.
That fire unites our will with the will of God,
so that two flames, the Flame of our love and the
    Flame of God,
become as one.
In this state the acts of love that we make
are all under God's influence and lift us
    heavenwards.

We learn from Scripture that:
"As your word unfolds it gives light" (Ps 119:130),
and "Does not your word burn like a fire?"
    (Jer 23:29).

Jesus himself said that his words were spirit and
    life (Jn 6:63).
People who love God
find God's words full of power,
whereas the mediocre find them insipid.

When Jesus announced the doctrine of
    the Eucharist
"many of his disciples left him" (Jn 6:66).
But others made a different response,
like Saint Peter who said:
"Lord, who shall we go to? You have the words
    of eternal life" (Jn 6:69).

The woman of Samaria too left her waterpots
and forgot her water
because of the sweetness of the Lord's words
(cf. Jn 4:28).
So when we have drawn close to God
through opening ourselves to God's Word,
we are transformed in the Flame which is the
Spirit,
and have a foretaste of everlasting life.

The Flame of God is said to be a "living" Flame
because it causes us to live spiritually in God
and makes us conscious of God's presence
within us.

And it is described as "wounding" because
God is continually touching us in numerous
ways,
like an ever-active fire, which burns unceasingly.
That fire can reach our inmost depths
where only the Holy Spirit dwells.

The more we love, the more deeply we enter into
God.
With even one degree of heat in our love
we move a little closer to God;
two degrees, three degrees, closer still.
But if we travel inwards as far as possible,

God can touch our inmost depths,
transforming us into the Divine.

God is our center,
and when we are living in our center
we have traveled as deeply into ourselves
    as possible.

At this point we are like a radiant and lucid
    crystal.
The more the crystal is in the light
the more luminous it becomes
until it seems to be light itself.

The Flame I am talking about as being burning
    and wounding
is also peaceful, tender and glorious.
It purifies us, making us crystal-clear,
and its sweetness transcends the fire of ordinary
    love,
since we burn in unison with the Flame that is
    God,
and not mere human love.

Purification Precedes Union

• • • • • •

When we began our spiritual journey
the Flame that touched us
was felt to be anything but sweet and peaceful,
because its work was to destroy
the imperfections and bad habits rampant
   within us.

It was the same Holy Spirit at work,
but the Spirit's effects were felt differently.
At the beginning they seemed very painful
   indeed,
whereas now they are felt to be sweet and
   pleasant.
Now there is a longing
for love to be perfected in the beatific vision.
It is as if the Holy Spirit
was inviting us to a new life in the words of the
   Canticle:

Come then, my love, my lovely one, come.
For see, winter is past,
the rains are over and gone.
The flowers appear on earth.
The season of glad songs has come.

The cooing of the turtledove is heard in our land.
The fig tree is forming its first figs
and the blossoming vines give out fragrance.
Come then my love, my lovely one, come.
My dove, hiding in the clefts of the rock,
in the coverts of the cliff,
show me your face, let me hear your voice;
for your voice is sweet and your face is beautiful
   (Song 2:10–14).

These words we now hear spoken within us by
   the Holy Spirit
in this sweet and tender Flame.
And therefore we can reply,
"Perfect your work if you so desire."

This basically contains the two requests
Jesus commanded us to make when he prayed,
"Your kingdom come, your will be done."
That is: "Give me your kingdom according to your
   will."
So we can continue to say, "Break the web of this
   sweet encounter,"
for we long for God to draw so close
that the web of life is broken
and we can see God face to face.

Other webs have been broken along the way,
such as the webs of created things

and the webs of merely natural desires and
  affections.
These have been gradually transformed and
  divinized
through the effects of a burning
that was painful and difficult to bear.

But as the web of life has become more diaphanous,
and the light of God has been able to shine
  through
to a greater and greater degree,
making us more like our divine Lover,
so we long for the final web that separates us from
  God to be broken.
Not cut or taken away gradually but actually
  broken.

This is quicker than waiting for time to run its
  course.

When we are burning with love
we long for its immediate consummation,
assailed and penetrated as we are by the fire of
  the Spirit.

Stanza 11

The Fire of Transforming Love

• • • • • •

O *sweet burn!*
O delicious wound!
O tender hand! O gentle touch!
Savoring of eternal life
And paying the whole debt.
In destroying death you have changed it into life.

The three persons of the Trinity, Father, Son, and
    Holy Spirit,
are all involved in the process of our transformation.

The *burn* is the Spirit,
the *hand* is the Father,
the *touch* is the Son.
In the second stanza of the poem
we praise the Father, Son, and Spirit
for all they have done for us,
all they have given us.

The first gift is the delicious wound or
burn that comes from the Spirit.
The second is the "taste of everlasting life"
that comes from the touch of the Son.

The third is the tender hand of the Father
as he gifts himself to us.
The persons of the Trinity, therefore, work
    together as one,
changing death into life.

Moses said, "The Lord your God is a consuming
    fire" (Dt 4:24).

That fire is a fire of love,
infinitely powerful and strong,
consuming all that stands in its way
and transforming it into itself.

But we are not all burned to the same degree.
It depends on our own preparation
as well as upon God's choice.

As the fire of love is infinite,
when it touches us its heat is more intense
than all the fires of this world.
It carries on burning until we not only feel the burn
but are wholly burnt up by the vehemence of the
    Flame.
In this way we are transformed into the Divine.

What a wonderful fire this is!
While it is strong enough
to burn up the whole world in its furnace

as easily as if it were a single straw,
yet it does not consume us
when we are enveloped in its flames.
Rather, it delights, deifies, and enlightens us
like the fire that descended on the disciples at
Pentecost.

The Spirit's coming is designed to lift us up,
to cheer us, delight us, and render us glorious.
It is indeed a sweet fire!
"The Spirit reaches the depths of everything, even
the depths of God" (1 Cor 2:10).
because it loves to search into all that belongs
to the One it loves.

Oh, happy are we when we are so loved and so
burned!
What a joy to be touched by this fire!
Even the wounding that this burn causes
is healed by the amazing love of the One who
inflicted it!

The Wound that Heals

• • • • • •

There is here a great paradox.
The more we are wounded the more healthy we
   are.
For the continued burning of love's fire
both heals and soothes even while it inflicts pain.
Indeed, the wounding is only present
in order that the Spirit may comfort us
more deeply and more abundantly.

O blessed wound inflicted by God who cannot
   but heal it!
O happy and blessed wound inflicted for our joy
   and comfort!
Great is the wound because of the greatness of
   the Inflictor!
Great is its delight — for love's fire is infinite!
This is indeed the touch of God!

Another way we can be burned
is when we are so set on fire
that we seem to be penetrated by a Seraph with a
   burning brand.
Then we feel love surging through every part of our
   being,

turning us into an immense sea of fire.
The tiny "mustard seed" of the kingdom
is coming to fruition as a "great tree."

This gift is sometimes given
to those who have a special work entrusted to
    them by God,
like the founders of religious Orders.

The wound of the Seraph may be shown outwardly
as in the stigmata of Saint Francis.
In such a case the natural pain felt in the flesh
is an outward sign of the love within.
There is sweetness in the midst of bitterness,
pleasure in the midst of pain.

Sometimes the wound is not manifest in any
    bodily way
but remains only an inner reality.
Thus we should not place too great an importance
    on the exterior,
and must beware of trying to force the body
in an effort to have some outward proof of our
    spirituality.
Real spirituality always works from the inside out,
not the other way around.

The Hand of God in Its
Transforming Work

· ● ● ● ● ·

The hand which inflicts these wounds of love
is a tender hand, extremely gentle in its touch,
yet able to annihilate the world
should it press down on creation.
Job felt this hand as hard. We feel it as gentle
and gracious.
And so we can pray in these words:

"To Job, Lord, you were severe,
while to me you are sweetness itself.
You never kill except to vivify.
You never wound except to heal.
Your touch is shown in your Son
who reveals your true nature to us.

"O gentle touch — O Word, very Son of God!
Because you are so pure
you can penetrate to the very substance of
    the soul!
O touch of the Word, so gentle and so strong.
You showed yourself to Elijah
in the whisper of the gentle breeze,

whereas before you had been breaking the rocks
in pieces.

"O strong and terrible Lord,
yet so gentle at the same time!
Most people ignore this whispering wind.
They will not listen to it.
They do not understand such deep matters.

"O God, purify me, for you are pure.
Hide me in the shelter of your wings.
Make me entirely your own.
Touch me, cleanse me, prepare me to receive You.
Change me into Yourself.
Only then can I know true joy."

Eternal Life Can Precede Bodily Death

· ● ● ● ● ● ·

We know, of course, that bodily death
precedes the vision of God in heaven.
But there is another life available to us
in which everything in us is God-directed,
and we live and act and think with the mind of
    God;
this is when everything within us and about us
is penetrated by the Spirit.
Then we are children of God in fact, not just in
    desire.
We are one with God
as a bride is one with her bridegroom in marriage.

In this state we seem to be keeping a perpetual
    feast of joy,
singing a new song,
delighting in all that is good and all that is of God.
We are conscious of God's tenderness and comfort,
and we know ourselves encouraged and
    engraced,
as if we were the only one in the world
for God to comfort, to care for, to provide for.
"My Beloved is mine and I am his" (Song 2:16).
What we experience in God's touch

is in some way a foretaste of everlasting life.
Some saints have known this
and could not find words to describe it,
so it is best to be silent.
It is something so personal
that it can belong only to the one who receives it,
like the "white stone" and new name
given to the elect in heaven (cf. Rv 2:17).

We may not be in heaven yet,
but in this state we share in the things pertaining
    to God:
fortitude, wisdom, love, beauty, grace, and
    goodness.
The "debt" that we had to pay
before we attained to the state of spiritual betrothal
was temptation, hardship, trials of mind and body,
so that spirit and flesh could be purified together.

More about the Process
of Purification

If we want to attain union with God,
we have, of necessity, to undergo times of testing
    and darkness.
Our spirit needs to be strengthened and the
    virtues refined,
just as iron is tested in the fire
and hammered into shape by the artist's hand.
The reason why more of us do not attain perfection
is because we do not cooperate with God
when God begins to work in us.
We want quick results, not the labor of patient
    endurance.
So God, realizing that we do not have the
    necessary courage,
stops testing us, and proceeds no further with our
    purification.
So we should count it a great favor
when we are tested through suffering.
We are God's favored children,
destined for union with the Divine even in this life,
if only we persevere.
Then the "death" that is inherent in suffering
will be changed into the life of glory even here
    below.

Stanza III

In Transforming Union We Share in God's Radiance

• • • • • •

O *lamps of fire,*
In whose splendors
The deep caverns of sense,
Which are usually dim and dark,
With an unusual brightness
Now give light and heat to the Beloved.

God will have to help me as I try to explain this
      verse;
and you, dear reader,
will need to pay careful attention to what I say,
as it may well seem rather obscure and difficult to
      understand.
Of course, if you have actually experienced what I
      write about,
then everything will be clear and full of joy.

In this stanza the bride-soul
thanks God for all she has received in the state of
      union.
Everything within her is now illumined by the fires
      of love,

and she responds by giving God
the very light and love that have been enkindled
    within her.
If we truly love, we are only satisfied when our
    whole self,
all that we have, are, and can be,
are offered to the One we love.
In this state we can radiate God's love,
which is communicated to us in unbelievable
    splendor;
and can joyfully offer that same love back to the
    Giver of all.

Lamps burn and give light;
and as God has so many attributes,
such as wisdom, love, omnipotence, mercy, and
    goodness,
so God reveals the divine essence to us
now in one way, now in another.

It is as if there are many lamps
and yet there is in reality only one lamp
burning and shining in numerous ways.

Moses knew the lamps of God
when God was seen by him on Sinai
as a God of "tenderness and compassion,
slow to anger, rich in kindness and faithfulness,
forgiving faults and sins,
yet leaving nothing unchecked" (Ex 34:6–7).

This is a most profound knowledge, the deepest
   delight of love.

The Bridegroom within us, being omnipotent,
gives himself to us and loves us omnipotently.
Being wise he loves us with wisdom,
being holy he loves us with holiness.
And as he is liberal,
he is always wanting to do good to us and give
   himself to us.

So how can I describe the feelings we have
when we know ourselves to be so loved and so
   honored?
Then we experience ourselves as being
like "a spring of living water
welling up to eternal life" (Jn 4:14).

Here the Spirit of God
is like sweet water hidden in our veins
and quenching our thirst.
The Spirit is also a living lamp of fire,
overflowing with love, acting with love,
and transforming us into the God who is love.

The Movements of the Spirit —
Ever Constant, Ever at Peace

• • • • • •

The splendor of love is communicated from within,
for the Spirit moves us to act and to love
as fire moves the air that is burning around it.

The movement and vibration of fire and flame
give us a foretaste of heavenly glory;
but paradoxically
there is a motionless center to the conflagration,
which is where God dwells as the immovable
    One.

God graces us with divine splendors,
but there is another word that can be used here
— the word "overshadowing."

To throw one's shadow over another person
signifies the giving of protection and favor.
Mary was told that she would be overshadowed
    by the Holy Spirit,
and would therefore partake of the Spirit's own
    life and power.

In this state the Spirit's shadow not only touches us
but makes us one with the Divine,
so that we rest secure in God's presence,
trusting and peaceful as Mary at the Annunciation.

The Purification of the Caverns Within Us

• • • • • •

The caverns within us are the powers of the soul:
memory, intellect, and will.
Their depths are commensurate with their
    capacity for good,
and only what is infinite can satisfy them.

When these caverns of intellect, memory, and will
    are impure
we are not conscious of our capacity to receive
    God.
We fill ourselves with trifling things that command
    our attention
and distract us from realizing our true dignity.

But once the caverns of memory, intellect, and will
    are emptied
and become aware of their emptiness,

as being possible receptacles for receiving divine
  love,
our sense of longing becomes intolerable.
The intellect longs for the waters of divine
  wisdom.
The will longs for the perfection of love.
The memory longs for the enjoyment of God.
And that longing is painful and insatiable.

But if the intellect, will, and memory
experience God in some degree, as indeed they
  do,
why is there so much pain in the process?
It is because there is a difference
between experiencing God by grace
and experiencing God by union.

It is like the difference between engagement and
  marriage.
Engagement implies mutual love, the giving of
  presents, visits,
but as yet there is no consummation
(although all that goes before has this end in view).

In the same way,
when we have attained to the state of betrothal,
and are secure in the love of God,
comforted by the visits and presents of our
  Bridegroom-to-be,

we can be unaware for a while
that more preparation is still needed before the
   wedding is celebrated.
The time of waiting increases our desire and longing.
But waiting is painful,
for consummation is so near and yet still seems so
   far away.
We have to complete our wedding preparations
and hold ourselves ready for the moment of union.
Let us not forget
that although we may be seeking God,
the Beloved is seeking us still more.

Everything is God's work above all.
It is important therefore not to put obstacles in
   God's way,
so that the Holy Spirit can lead us unimpeded
   along the path of faith.

God Alone Must Be Our Guide

· · ● ● ● ● · ·

If at this crucial time we put ourselves
into the hands of people who do not understand
the ways of God,
we will be hindered on our journey.
For example, we find that we cannot pray now as
we used to do
when we practised meditation
and experienced sweet feelings in prayer.
It is time to renounce the desire for pleasant
    sensations
and allow God to guide us along a secret and
uncharted route.

We need to be free,
encouraging an inner disposition
of passive, loving attention in prayer:
detached, serene, silent.
We must be like the atmosphere
which the sun warms and illuminates
in proportion to its calmness and purity.
Others may try to tell us otherwise, but they are
    wrong.

We must not listen to blind guides
who try to force us along other paths;
hammering us into shapes of their own designing
like unskilled blacksmiths.

We should not try to understand ourselves either.
In this state it is pure waste of time.
We must be like a child resting in our mother's arms,
not crying and struggling to walk unaided
before we are ready.
God is carrying us like a mother,
even though we are not aware of going anywhere.
In fact, we *are* going somewhere,
although we are not conscious of the fact.

Let us abandon ourselves into God's hands.
If we do this we advance securely.
There is only danger when we try to act on our
  own resources.

The Practice of Contemplation

· ● ● ● ● ● ·

To be attentive to God
we must be completely self-forgetful,
intent only on listening to the One who speaks to us.
Contemplation means receiving;
and we cannot receive unless we are empty,
prepared to accept whatever God wishes to say
and do with us.

If we take the log and speck from our own eye
then the sun will shine for us and enable us to see
    clearly.
Then God, the unsleeping keeper of Israel,
will shine upon our emptiness
and fill us with good things.

We have to remain in solitude
under the influence of the Holy Spirit;
then we will be taken care of,
being given consolation or desolation as God
    pleases.

The Difference between Darkness and Blindness

• • • • • •

There are two possible reasons why we cannot see:
either we are in the dark or we are blind.
Blindness proceeds from sin,
darkness not necessarily so.

When God does not shine on us we are in
    darkness
even though we may have faultless vision otherwise.
When we are mired in sin then we are blind,
and even if God's light is shining on us
we are still unable to see.
On the other hand, we can be in darkness
in that we are unaware of spiritual values
until God enlightens us.
Little by little God wants us to choose light over
    darkness,
choose sight over blindness.
We must learn to desire light and sight.
That means realizing the true worth of things and
    people,
rather than judging them merely by how they
    affect us
on a natural level.

If we are not careful we will identify God
with passing pleasure and beautiful feelings.
God must be desired for Godself alone.
If we desire God we will leave natural desires
    aside
and not confuse things of the senses with the
    things of God.
Then the caverns within us
will truly give light and heat to the Beloved.

Becoming Light from Contact
with the Divine Light

In the state of union
the caverns of the soul — memory, intellect, and will
— are like lamps that have been lighted by God
and are burning in God.

Our senses are naturally dim and dark
until they are purified;
but as we advance we become light in the Lord.
The caverns of the senses begin to give out light
    and heat,
transforming us, and making it possible for us
to give God love for love.

We can even give God to God,
since it is God's gifts that enable us to shine and
glow, as crystals reflect the rays of the sun.

Here every debt is paid
for we reflect God back to God.
We gift God with the gifts given us.
We take intense delight in loving God
with the Spirit who dwells within us.
Memory, intellect, and will
now unite in praise of God and in joy even in
this life.
There is a mutual interchange of love
as in the surrender of marriage,
each giving him or herself up to the other.
This makes us supremely happy.
We live enlightened by faith and enkindled by
love,
loving God for who God is, not what God gives.
But the way there
means taking on and living through darkness
as part of the package.

Stanza IV

Awakening to Love's Consummation

• • • • • •

How gently and how lovingly
You lie awake in my heart
Where you dwell secretly and alone;
And in your sweet breathing,
Full of grace and glory,
How tenderly you fill me with love.

Here we can turn toward the Bridegroom
with great love and thanksgiving for two effects
which God sometimes gives those
who have reached the state of union.

The first effect
is the way God awakens us through love and
   gentleness.
The second effect is the breathing of God within us
by way of grace and glory.
This makes us love God very sweetly and tenderly.
It is as if we were awakening from sleep and
   drawing breath,
knowing that the Lord abides within us
in a close and intimate union.

We can say in a paraphrase of the above stanza:
Oh, how gently and lovingly
you lie awake in the center of my soul,
where you dwell secretly and alone in silence.

You abide in me as my sole Lord,
not only as if in your own house and your own
    room,
but also within my heart in close and intimate
    union.

Oh, how gently and lovingly you are present!
Sweet to me is your breathing in that awakening
for it is full of grace and glory.
Oh, with what tenderness you inspire me to love
    you!

God Makes Us Aware of the Beauty
of All Creation

• • • • • •

There are numerous ways in which God awakens
   us,
but what I am describing here is what, in my
   opinion,
is the highest kind of awakening.
It is the awakening that comes
from a movement of the Word, the Son of God,
in our very depths.
This is an awakening that makes it seem
as if all the balsams, fragrant herbs, and flowers of
   the world,
were mingled and shaken together
to produce a rare and indefinable sweetness.

The whole world looks different,
even creation seems changed and charged with
   goodness.

This is because God bears all creation within
   Godself;
and in coming to us
reveals creation's true inner beauty and loveliness.

For creation is rooted in God,
and from God draws its life and being.

At this point we know creation in God,
rather than knowing God through creation.
The veil which conceals God seems to be drawn
    back,
(though not the veil of faith
which will always remain in this life),
and we are enabled to behold the beauty
that surrounds us and is within us.
We cannot do this of ourselves;
it is God's work and God's gift.

The result of this "awakening of the heart"
lets us then cry out with longing:
Awake and enlighten us, Lord,
that we may know and love
the good things you have set before us.
Awaken us that we may know that you wish to do
    us good,
and that you remember us always!

God Enables Us to Bear
the Beams of Love

• • • • • •

But how can we bear
to hold God and creation within our own being
while we are still in this mortal flesh?
Why do we not faint away, as Esther nearly fainted
when she looked upon the glory of the king, her
    husband (Ex 15:7–13)?

It is because God's greatness and glory
are shown to us with love and tenderness
rather than with awe and terror.
We are protected from being overwhelmed by the
    divine glory
as Moses was protected by the hand of God
    (Ex 33:22).

In this state we are strengthened
to sustain the depths of joy that we feel
in knowing God as our Spouse and Brother.
In such a relationship of love all fear is banished.
We know ourselves to be as a queen,
and this knowledge comes to pass in the depths of
    our soul
where God dwells secretly all alone.

The Ways in which God Dwells
Within Us in This Life

• • • • • •

We have to keep in mind that God dwells
in secret and hidden ways in all people and all
    things,
for if God did not do so they could not exist at all.

But the dwelling of God in us is different,
according to our personal dispositions
and according to our response to grace.

In some God dwells alone, in others not.
In some God dwells content, in others displeased.
In some God dwells as in a home
which is ruled and ordered by the Divine
    Indweller,
while in others God is not permitted to do
    anything at all.
Where personal desires and self-will least abound,
there God is most alone and contented.
There God can dwell as in a home
belonging totally to the Divinity.

The more secretly God dwells within us,
the more God is the sole Lover and Master.

So then, if we have ceased to desire any specific
    thing,
and have cast out all created forms and images,
the Beloved can dwell most secretly within us.
And the purer we are,
the more estranged from anything that is not God,
the more we are open to God's close embrace
    and intimacy
in a way that not even Satan can penetrate.
Oh, blessed are we when we are ever conscious of
    God
resting and reposing within us!
How necessary for us to try to remain in tranquility
    of spirit.
God must be allowed to sleep within us,
for were God always awake we could not sustain
    the impact,
and would enter into eternal glory.

If we have not yet attained to this state of union,
God nevertheless dwells secretly within us also;
but we are usually unconscious of the divine
    presence.
However, we may be conscious of it occasionally
and in a less tranquil manner.

Conclusion

· • • • • · ·

In awakening to union
it is as if we were awakening from sleep and drawing
    breath;
and, while doing so,
feeling the sweet breathing of God within us.

I cannot speak of this breathing,
neither do I want to.
Anything I say could barely approximate the reality;
for here God breathes the Holy Spirit into us
in deepest mystery.

This breathing, full of grace and glory,
fills those who are open to receive it.
In this experience the Holy Spirit inspires us
with a love of God that surpasses all understanding.

For this reason I must desist
from speaking further on the subject.

Also available in the same series:

Teresa of Avila's *The Way of Perfection* ... *for Everyone*

Elizabeth Ruth Obbard

In the sixteenth century Teresa of Avila wrote *The Way of Perfection,* an introduction to life and prayer for her young Carmelite novices as they set out on the contemplative path. This re-telling of her classic in modern idiom makes her core teachings accessible to contemporary readers who feel called to a deeper, more God-centered life. Teresa, a doctor of the church, sets out the principles and practice of the life of prayer that can speak to *you* as you journey with God in your own life.

64 pages, paperback
ISBN: 978-1-56548-262-3

Thérèse of Lisieux's "Little Way" ... *for Everyone*

Elizabeth Ruth Obbard

Thérèse is loved by many. And deservedly so. This unassuming nun has been made a doctor of the Church because her words have brought comfort and wisdom to people of all ages everywhere. The simplified vocabulary and sentence structure of this book make her thoughts available with art and gracefulness. *Thérèse of Lisieux's "Little Way" for Everyone* will delight and nourish all who read it.

72 pages, paperback
ISBN: 978-1-56548-272-2

To order call 1-800-462-5980 or
e-mail orders@newcitypress.com